Ra Press
100 Kennedy Drive #53
South Burlington, Vt. 05403

ISBN  978-1-365-28507-3

# Adirondack Epiphanies

Linda Morrow
Mary L. Randall
Charles Watts
Cathy S. McDowell
Chuck Gibson
Judith Dow Moore

# Table of Contents

**Hold My Hand We're Almost There** *Mary L. Randall*
**Eager to Fall from the Peak** *Charles Watts*
  *(a sestina)*
**The Boat** *Cathy S. McDowell*

**Autumn Sequence** *Judith Dow Moore*
*It Begins*
*Pied Autumn*
*Cold Earth Wanderers*
*Burning Bush*
*At Ricky's*
*Champlain Surface with Clouds*
*My Mother's Pictures*
*Autumn with Drought*
*All the Colors start to Fade*
*Afterward*

**Interlude** *Linda Morrow*
**Ever So Slightly** *Cathy S. McDowell*
**Nine Sonnets** *Chuck Gibson*
*Lost Pond*
*Saranac Lake, Fourth of July*
*Lincoln Pond*
*Long Pond*
*When I was Leaving Church in the Foyer*
*Champlain*
*Ausable Flume*
*Discovery Mountain*
*Upper Boquet*

**Sun Tea** *Cathy S. McDowell*
**2 Haikus** *Mary L. Randall*
**The Nature of Place** (*a paean to Placid*) *Charles Watts*

*"Gratitude bestows reverence, allowing us to encounter everyday epiphanies, those transcendent moments of awe that change forever how we experience life and the world."*

**John Milton**

# HOLD MY HAND
## AND WE'RE HALFWAY THERE
*Mary L. Randall*

As a child in the 60s, I spent summers in Lake Luzerne. On rainy days I listened to record albums, including soundtracks of musicals my parents had seen on Broadway. Going to shows was a great treat for them and they brought home LPs of *Camelot, Man of La Mancha, Fiddler on the Roof, My Fair Lady, West Side Story, The Sound of Music, Funny Girl...* I played those records over and over and over until I learned every song by heart. I sing them still as I drive around the Adirondacks. The work I do requires way too much time spent in the car. Recently, I dodged a deer that ran out in front of me on Chilson Hill, as I was singing, "If Ever I Would Leave You." The irony was not lost on me - as the deer had been "running merrily through the snow." Musical scores made me a poet, honed my memory and filled me with the thrill of exercising memory to master a skill. Each person's head is a storage shed that can become a treasure trove, a vast wilderness or a junk heap. Pay attention to what you keep upstairs.

When it wasn't raining, I walked along with my siblings to the beach, uphill past the Hilltop Store, whose motto was *On the hill but on the level*. They sold groceries, candy, comic books, ammunition, fishing tackle, lucky rabbit's foot key chains, and you could buy a fudgsicle for seven cents. As we walked, I always scanned the woods, hoping to spot a deposit bottle that I could cash in at the Hilltop. We walked the rest of the way to the small beach on the lake, where we spent most of each day. Every now and then a busload of city kids would arrive and run screaming into the water, thrashing about with wild delight. I stood in the shallows up to my knees, watching the *fresh air* kids, and I began to sing, "There's a Place for us," without even realizing I was doing it. One of the kids stopped and turned and looked at me when he heard, "Peace and quiet and open air wait for us somewhere." He swam over and stood before me as I kept on singing. This lucky boy received my first private concert offered to a stranger. His wet skin was the color of a Hershey bar, his smile was bright, astonished, and his eyes gleamed as he asked, "Who *are* you?" The counselor in the lake with the other kids called out to him before I could answer. She hollered, "Ricky, come and stay with the group!" I never got to tell him my name and soon the counselor rounded them up, they boarded the bus and away they went. I can close my eyes and see Ricky's face before me, smiling still as he wonders how a young kid could be singing that song, maybe a song he had heard, maybe a song he would hear in the future and it would bring him back to that beach in the mountains, to being a happy boy in a lake that held more than fish and water, that held spells cast by sound and sense, by Leonard Bernstein and Stephen Sondheim.

I never tried to join a chorus or band. I never acted in a musical, nor stood on a stage to perform. It did not occur to me to approach it from that direction. I simply like to memorize lyrics and entertain myself by reciting or singing, whether or not I can be overheard.

When I was in high school they put on *Fiddler* and a boy I knew who stuttered terribly was cast in the role of Motel, who loves Tzeitel. I could not believe that Billy was expected to speak, let alone sing. All of us had heard him try to answer questions in class that seemed to last forever as he battled his speech impediment and we silently cringed. I gave him credit for his attempts at public speaking but I thought the music and drama teacher cruel to place Billy in this position, under a spotlight. The first performance was on a Friday afternoon - just for the students and teachers. When Billy strode onto the stage he walked with confidence that stunned me. His red hair shone beneath the lights. I never knew another kid with such an impressive level of personal bravery. All of us held our breath when he opened his mouth and belted out the song *Wonder of Wonders*. As he sang the ending, "But of all God's miracles large and small / the most miraculous one of all / is the one I thought could never be / God has given you to me!" we leapt to our feet, screaming and cheering. Never, ever have I been to any other performance where the audience went crazy as we did when we heard our own Billy singing like a nightingale. I later learned that singing is a technique that helps people who stutter to overcome that obstacle, but that afternoon in the auditorium, I sat among my peers as we witnessed what seemed to be a true miracle.

*Thank you, Jerry Bock and Sheldon Harnick.*

The life I chose led me to "fight the unbeatable foe" and to "bear with unbearable sorrow." This is the path of the crusader for social justice, where the road is always uphill. Indeed, I have "marched into hell for a heavenly cause." It is good to have a theme song that steadies your nerves and strengthens your resolve.

*Thank you, Dale Wasserman, Mitch Leigh and Joe Darion.*

When I was five years old, my Dad took me along with two of my older sisters to a matinee performance of *The Sound of Music*. He picked me up at school and away we went, as we lived on the island back then and Manhattan was not far off. It was Mary Martin's understudy who sang the lead that afternoon. What I could never get out of my head was the question posed at the end of *"How Do You Solve a Problem like Maria?"* And that is, "How do you hold a moonbeam in your hand?"

*Thank you, Richard Rodgers and Oscar Hammerstein. And thank you to the understudy whose name I do not know, as women hold up half the sky (or is it 51 percent?)*

And who can ever forget Eliza Doolittle and Professor Henry Higgins? "Now once again, where does it rain? / In Spain! In Spain! / And where's that blasted plain? / In Spain! In Spain!" The hilarious song, *"Why Can't a Woman Be More Like a Man?"* boosted me to the next level, as I ran around the Luzerne house chasing and singing at the little kids, who screeched with merriment, "If I were a woman who'd been to a ball / been hailed as a princess by one and by all / would I start weeping like a bathtub overflowing? / Or carry on as if my home were in a tree? / would I run off and never tell me where I'm going? / Why can't a woman be like me?"

*Thank you, George Bernard Shaw, Frederick Lowe, Alan Jay Lerner, even the much maligned Marni Nixon, whose voice was dubbed into the movie, replacing the loverly Audrey Hepburn, whom I adored.*

Barbra Steisand upped the bar for everyone by doing it all: singing, acting, writing, directing. The professor who taught Shakespeare at my college had been Ms. Streisand's high school English teacher. When she told him of her chosen career path; to become a star on Broadway, he thought she was kidding herself - first of all, the nose. He did not have good instincts. Fast-forward from being wrong about Ms. Streisand, he predicted a bright future for me as a scholar. Unlike many divas that did not go on to star in the film version after she had knocked them dead on Broadway,

Streisand charted her own course. When she sings, "I want to live and live now / Get what I want, I know how / I'm an American Beauty Rose / with and American beauty nose / eye on the target and wham! / one shot, one gunshot and BAM / Hey Mr. Arnstein, here I am!" she is not kidding.

*Thank you, Isobel Lennart, Jule Styne and Bob Merrill. Much credit is also due to Jerome Robbins who said, "You can't cast Mary Martin in this role. You need a Jewish girl." When Carol Burnett was offered the role, she echoed Robbins' advice.*

We are shaped by our times and by wherever it is we land. The actor, Jack Nicholson, grew up with his grandmother playing the role of his mother and his mother playing the role of his adoring sister. Back when he was born, in 1937, an unwed pregnant showgirl had to disappear from the face of the earth. Elaborate fictions were contrived. She might be sent off to help an ailing aunt who was recovering from surgery in a distant city, even if she did not have an aunt. Meanwhile, her own mother would pretend to be pregnant - oldest trick in the book.

I take great comfort in the treasury of song that is lodged between my ears. Reciting sonnets in the car as I drove my young daughter to school thirty-six years ago, I would stop speaking at the end of each line, before saying the last word or two, and she would instantly fill that in. It is a beautiful memory for both of us.

# EAGER TO FALL FROM THE PEAK
### *(a sestina)*
*Charles Watts*


Twisting his head to see the peak
Before beginning the slow hike
Around the lake prior to the climb
To and above the treeline trudge
To and above the screeline slide
He could only think of the last fall

His lover took, the lingering fall
From when their passion hit its peak
Only to begin the long last slide
That no amount of caring could hike
The road that neither choose to trudge
With no hills left for them to climb

It began on their first together climb
Back before the leaves announced fall
A slow and mostly focused trudge
To  find if us was near the peak
A mountain stream to end the hike
Into which they both could slide

Their clothing on the bank, they slide
Into the water and begin their climb
Into each other, washing off the hike
Letting the wreckage of the past fall
As if their love had not reached its peak
As if their love had not become a trudge

Both knowing, the long and bitter trudge
Back home turned into a darkling slide
As they stumbled back from the peak
Of passion that colored their climb

The gray boredom that cushioned the fall
From this, the last tramp, the last hike

One last time they embraced, to hike
The stakes, to shake off the bitter trudge
But nothing could stand in the way of their fall
From grace, nothing could interrupt the slide
From ease to emptiness that ended their climb
Just before they finally reached the peak

He dreamed the hike was worth the slide
She made the trudge home, made the climb
Into bed, eager to fall from the peak

## THE BOAT
*Cathy S. McDowell*


When my dad was first diagnosed with Alzheimer's, the doctor asked him to write a sentence. A few minutes later he took the paper back and read the sentence. My dad had written, "God is Love".

Only time gives clarity. I have come to understand that life is just a series of circles opening and then closing.

I remember an Indian summer night in early September about ten years ago. It had been a crazy day at work. I was stressed. Around 7:30 that evening, I told Dad I was going down to the lake to swim laps - something I often did to chill out and get back some peace.

My father said, "No, I think it's too late for you to be down there alone." I remember it really bothered me that he didn't think I could take care of myself. Especially since I was 52 at the time. I told him I was going anyway.

The lake was still and smooth. I was the only one in the bay since all the summer people had left. I'd lost track of time and I was still swimming laps back and forth between our dock and Rocky Point at 8:15. I was alone. The water was black now.

As I touched Rocky Point and headed back for my last lap, I saw something floating to the left of me in the water. It was a little boat with my dad in it. He had been rowing along next to me the whole time.

I think my father was like God. Sometimes loving me from a distance because I think I know how to do everything without Him. But he was always there, even in the dark parts, loving, protecting and teaching.

I was with my father when he died. And I got the chance to complete a circle of love and row next to him while he completed his final lap.

# AUTUMN SEQUENCE

## *10 poems*

*In my poems I try to communicate not only the beauty of what I sense, but also the spirit and enchantment of it.*

*Judith Dow Moore*

## It Begins

Then in an August minute
Everything changes
The sleek green pelts of the summer hills
Become the rough calico coats of
Autumn
Not yet vulpine reds or leonine yellows
But mottled infinite shadings of
Greenyellowbrownblackpurplegold
Bluefawn…
And the air no longer somnolent
Becomes acerb,astonished,attentive

## Pied Autumn

I love the pale colors of autumn massed
Against a field, a hill, the sky.
Even the despised sumac assumes the soft red
Of Renaissance dress.
The infinite shadings of green,
The subtle purples of the wild asters ,
The muted yellows, hushed browns play
A sinuous harlequinade in the dreamy
October haze.

I have picked up two leaves - No two are alike.
Green gone, they revert to their essential colors.
One bronze with red overtones and scarlet
lower lobe
The other with drifting continents of gold
and gray.
They have given their gifts of shade and breath
And now their last gifts of desiccated beauty
Soon to crumble and to return their
elements to earth.

How I envy this soft and beautiful dispersal
The lovely process from bud back to beginnings
My gifts given freely, I too would like to cancel
All ugly fuss and simply dissolve into mist,
Or wind blown leaves or the warm earth.

## Cold Earth Wanderers

The church was dark after autumn sun
Two children stood, one on each side of the aisle.
The boy on the right guarding the donation basket
The girl on the left handing out concert programs.
Under the ceiling lights their hair was gold over dark,
Faces like the stained glass angels behind them,
Surrounding the green cloak of St. Patrick.

Then the music. The cellist, tall,
frail, white haired
The children's mother playing the grand piano
Bodies entangled in the
rhythms that ran through them
Branched rafters magnifying, returning the sound.
First a duet, challenge, response, resolution
Then the cellist's own composition.
No one knows his age.
But the music was from the earth's beginning.

After intermission, the boy, restless
Went out into the warm afternoon sun.
He found the magical five-legged tree,
an ancient elder
Sprawled on the grass, he dreamed a story
About five hungry animals.
What should they do?
"Follow the elephant," he said aloud,
and walked back.
The piano and the cello were playing Delius.

## Burning Bush

Late one October Afternoon
a season-slanted sun lit
a tangle of wild asters, thistles
bare raspberry canes.
Purple flowers burned
with monarch butterflies, hornets, wasps.
With gold fretted wings
life buzzed and flamed.
Children's heads were warm under our hands,
Sun never shone before in just this way.
Like tiny moons, waxing and waning
the monarchs' wings
shifted from dark to light.
The rhythmic hum of golden
insects grew to fill the air
as we gazed shocked into
knowing the power,
the mystery
in weeds, in light, in life.

## At Ricky's

Is the smoke coming from the chimney?
Can you see a light?
Is Ricky's old tan panel truck there?
Yes? Then it's open; it's all right.

It's a treasure cave, is Ricky's place
The gloom welcomes you.
The crowd up front hides the beer
As you walk through.

Stacks of musty books and dusty pictures
Shelves of plate and glass
Furniture hidden by old things
That clutch you as you pass.

At Ricky's are scraps of my childhood
An ugly old dresser, a rhinestone pin
A crazy quilt of the forties, the fifties
And the memories flood in

 I love going to Ricky's emporium
To buy a glimpse of time lost
In an old enamel kitchen table
And at so small a cost.

It's near the interstate exit
Go past the chuck wagon painted red
(from a cowboy theme park of long ago.)
It's magic, just as I said.

## Champlain Surface with Clouds

Off the north shore
Ebony water gleams
Mirrors trees of
Somber pensive yellow.
Here, the landing site's
Grass and concrete
Are chalky with bird dung.

Water rolls slowly
Like a great beast waking
Surface slick like
Pale brown silk, so clear.
Each yellow leaf on the bottom,
A Japanese wood block
Clouds overhead
Make ghosts in the water
Ectoplasmic limbs
Reaching, receding.

## My Mother's Pictures

From Norway, my mother chose for her bedroom
Edvard Munch's <u>Girls on a Jetty.</u>
One bareheaded in white, one in a red cloak,
one in green.
All gazing into the scene reflected in the harbor
At the phallic shadow of the twilight tree
Dwarfing the full moon and pale houses,
blackening the water.

In our dining room, Van Gogh's <u>La Berceuse</u>
Dreamed the universe, cradle rope
slack in kind hands
Deep in trancelike thought, she gazed inward
Full breasts modest in dark green
above wide skirts
Colored like sunlit grass,
the floor beneath blood red,
Her head crowned by starry flowers
on dark wallpaper.

Pink and yellow desert light blazed from
Diego Rivera's <u>Sleeping Child</u>`
(Behind a red chair in the living room.)
The child's form curved behind a doll
Shaped like a grown woman on the left.
"His mother-tossed away," my mother quipped.
On the extreme right a flowered sugar skull
Gazed dispassionately.

## Autumn Drought

Between lake and land
A continent has emerged
Naked slime and sand

The mallards skirt gingerly the wreaths
Of glaucous, oozy algae,
Finding sustenance beneath

Champlain droops under her curdled coat
Perhaps that is why she is deserted
By all but one moored sailboat.

Patience. The awaited autumn rains
Will wash away the stains.

## All the Colors Start to Fade

In the middle I have stayed
Through long years until at last
All the colors start to fade

With scarlet flags in life's parade
Friends have beckoned as they passed
In the middle I have stayed

Though before me earth has laid
Rainbow treasures long amassed
All the colors start to fade

Blood dark games I never played
Death's bright dice I feared to cast
In the middle I have stayed

Fire of opal, ice of jade
Flickering love, extinguished fast
All the colors start to fade

Memories like debts unpaid
Strands of grayness veil the past
In the middle I have stayed
All the colors now must fade.

## Afterward

Light
     in a house
          intensely lived in
dims when that life leaves.
The table where she always sat, is just a table, an
"antique",
   Venetian gondolas in a picture --
                   no longer luminous.
The yellow pottery is dull and chipped.
Photographs of oddly dressed strangers
          topple on the mantle.
The gifts of light--shadow, sharpness, dimension--
               diminish
   Leaving flat thin in corporeality.

**INTERLUDE**

*Linda Morrow*

INTERLUDE is excerpted from my "in progress" memoir, about raising a son born with Down syndrome in 1966, at a time when services and support were difficult to access.

*"You cannot stay on the summit forever; you have to come down again. So why bother in the first place? Just this: What is above knows what is below, but what is below does not know what is above. One climbs, one sees. One descends, one sees no longer, but one has seen. There is an art of conducting oneself in the lower regions by the memory of what one saw higher up. When one can no longer see, one can at least still know."*

*— <u>René Daumal</u>*

Whack! Crack! Thump! Splash! Seated in the bow of an aluminum Grumman canoe, my right hand gripped the metal shaft of the paddle just above the throat while my left clamped onto the T-shaped handle. Like a laborer operating a pile driver, I slammed the polypropylene blade onto the puddled slurry ice covering the surface of Long Lake, deep in the heart of upstate New York's Adirondack Park. In the stern, my paddling partner flipped aside floating ice cakes with her blade and whooped and hollered as she pushed our vessel through the narrow line of open water. Strung out behind us followed ten more women in five canoes – silver links on a blue chain. In early May of 1978, winter clung stubbornly to the glacial lakes dotting this remote wilderness.

--------------

We'd met for the first time two mornings ago at the Dartmouth Outward Bound Center (DOBC) located on the Dartmouth College campus in Hanover, NH. We were all members of Course #D-54, just the Center's second course created for women over thirty. For ten days we would carry everything we needed on our collective backs – food, shelter, basic amenities (read toilet paper) as we disengaged from our busy, complex lives. We would paddle our canoes along lakes and rivers and portage on well-worn trails and untrammeled wilderness for over 50 miles.

Some of us had paid ($325.00) for this privilege; some received scholarships. All of us had our own reasons for choosing this adventure: love of nature, recovery, a new experience, a testosterone-free environment. I wanted to test myself physically and escape the responsibilities of being a mother to three active boys – ages eleven, ten and seven - as well as my wifely obligations.

We'd camped at Storrs Pond, on the outskirts of town, the first night – way too close to home for me – and cooked our first meal over a campfire; the spaghetti and meat sauce tasted delicious. Racing against the impending darkness, we split up into tent groups and received instruction on the art of pitching our four-person tents. As I lay in my sleeping bag, adrenaline pulsing through my body, I thought about the last eight months - they'd flown by so quickly.

In late August our family had left the hustle and bustle of Long Island and settled in the bucolic beauty of Hanover, New Hampshire. My husband's sabbatical from his position at SUNY-Stony Brook coupled with my desire to return to my New England roots drove our move. I had looked forward to a year in this ivy-league college town. I wanted to expose my two youngest sons

Mike and Josh to the activities I'd relished as a child – downhill skiing, looking at a miniature world from a mountain summit, paddling down a river, jumping from a boulder into the bracing clear water of a lake. But more importantly was the opportunity for our oldest son Steve, born with Down syndrome, to attend the same elementary school as his brothers – something he'd never done. New federal legislation, along with the willingness of Hanover's Ray School to accept the challenges of mainstreaming, had made this possible.

Now, as the time to return to our home in Port Jefferson, NY drew closer, I'd begun to experience a significant amount of internal conflict, resulting in distraction and depression. I didn't want to leave a place I'd grown to love. I didn't want to return to the strip-mall commercial development and materialistic culture of Long Island. And I didn't want Steve to go back to his segregated, self-contained class of special-needs students run by the Bureau of Cooperative Educational Services (BOCES) and located each year in whatever central Suffolk County school had available space. I tossed and turned on my narrow Therm-A-Rest pad and struggled to untangle my legs and feet from the narrow confines of my sleeping bag. Eventually, I shut off my brain and drifted off to sleep.

The following morning, I sat cross-legged on the ground staring at the steam rising from a gelatinous light-brown mass I'd spooned into the tin cup which would serve as my all-purpose eating and drinking container for the next nine days.

"What exactly is this?" I asked Dorcas, the assistant instructor. "It doesn't look or smell like oatmeal."

"You're right. This is a whole-wheat grain originating from the Middle East called bulgur, very healthy, give it a try."

I did. "Eck! It's like eating sawdust!"

"Well, get used to the taste. Bulgur is our breakfast staple for the trip."

I immediately christened the grain, "vulgar bulgur."

A DOBC van transported us across the Connecticut River to a nearby cliff. There, under azure skies, puffy white clouds and a warming sun, we spent several hours at the base of an exposed granite cliff learning to climb and rappel using harnesses and ropes. Unlike the canoe expedition which would form the backbone of the course, figuring out a path up the steep rock face was a completely new experience for me and I delighted in the challenge.

Around 4 pm we departed for our next campsite, leaving behind the familiar environs of the Hanover area. For seven hours, my excitement increased as we traveled over pot-holed back country roads in a wheezing van piloted by a DOBC driver. A trailer with six canoes rattled behind us and the mound of gear piled high on the roof rack gave the van the appearance of a lumbering oversized turtle. We stopped only once, for gas. Dinner came in a large pot containing cold, leftover bulgur with chopped onion and carrots and cubes of cheese added in. The pot was passed around and each of us scooped out handfuls of the revolting mix.

Finally, we staggered, stiff-legged, out of the van into a cold driving rain. Flashlights, clenched in our mouths, cut the inky darkness as we hurried to unload the gear and canoes. Caught in the headlights' bright beams, the rain seemed to intensify as the driver backed up the van and swung out of the campground – probably headed for a warm, dry motel room. Frantically, we struggled to pitch our tents, dug for our inflatable mattress pads and sleeping bags, and hastily crawled, soaking wet, into already sagging tents. Ahead of us stretched a six day expedition along a water route once traveled by Native Americans, fur trappers and traders.

Early the next morning, I crawled out of our drooping tent, stood, and looked around. Before me, surrounded by towering pines, stretched Long Lake, aptly named for its fourteen mile length. Tendrils of steaming mist rose in a blue-bird sky as the sun's warm rays heated the cold waters. A slight breeze sent wavelets lapping at the graveled shore.

After breakfast, Nancy, the head instructor, and Dorcas lined us up shoulder to shoulder with paddles in hand and began an introduction to various essential strokes. The bow paddler needed to know the forward stroke to propel the canoe forward; and the draw and cross-draw strokes to turn the canoe quickly. The woman in the stern used the J stroke to keep the canoe on a center line and the stern pry stroke for turning. With both paddlers on the same side, a sculling stroke moved the canoe sideways across the water – an effective way to cozy up parallel to other canoes – known as "rafting-up."

For me and a couple of the other women, none of this information was new. I'd learned to canoe at lake-side sleep-a-way camps in northern Vermont and then, as a counselor, taught canoeing for three years at a YWCA camp on Lake Winnipesaukee in New Hampshire. But on the first morning, those of us with experience kept our mouths shut. Everyone has to learn sometime!

"OK, ladies, that's enough," called out Nancy, a lanky woman with lively blue eyes. A smile split her high cheek-boned face. She pulled her long brunette hair into a careless pony tail and jammed a red toque on her head. "Pair off, grab a life jacket and let's get on the water!"

I turned to the woman standing next to me. "Your name's Sheila, right? Do you want to paddle with me today?" She gave a slight nod. Beneath her dark, curly hair, her eyes had a hooded, furtive cast and her face seemed pinched by a deep hidden pain. (Later I gained a new respect for Sheila when she shared that after a breakdown and hospitalization on the psychiatric ward of Hanover's Dartmouth Hitchcock hospital, the trip was part of her recovery plan.) We rummaged through the pile of hunter-orange life jackets, each looking for the right size.

"Each pair needs to carry a canoe down to the water and meet Nancy and me there," called Dorcas. Shorter and more serious than Nancy, Dorcas had covered her short bowl-cut brown hair with a red bandana knotted at the back of her neck. She stood hands on her hips, legs spread apart and the bottoms of her khaki canvas pants stuffed into shin-high scuffed olive-green rubber boots.

A row of aluminum canoes, about fifty feet from the shoreline, lay keel-side-up, tilted to one side, like giant cans of sardines. As we walked toward the last canoe in the line, Sheila spoke, "I've never canoed before, have you?"

"Yeah," I admitted. "I have."

"Oh," she replied meekly, "I hope you aren't sorry you asked me to paddle with you."

"No, not at all," I answered.

Down at the lake's edge, Nancy and Dorcas demonstrated the proper technique for getting in a canoe. Carrying the bow, Dorcas waded into the ankle-numbing water. *So that's why she's wearing rubber high-tops,* I thought. Nancy lowered the stern so it rested on the sand.

"You're probably all wishing you had Dorcas's boots right now," she chortled. "They're not much of a fashion statement, but they do work! As for me, I just wade in with these hiking boots. They're water proof... sort of."

Then Nancy placed her legs on either side, or gunwale, of the boat and clamped the stern with her knees. She reached forward with her hands to further steady the canoe. "The stern paddler functions as the captain, and the bow person doesn't enter until she gets the OK from the stern," she declared. "All set, Dorcas."

Dorcas nodded toward Nancy and reached for the far gunwale with one hand and the near gunwale with the other. "Once you get the OK, you want to position yourself like I've done. Step with the same leg as your far hand into the center of the canoe, stay low and follow with your other leg." As she lifted each leg, she gave a shake before swinging it into the canoe. "This way you avoid collecting water on the bottom. Helps keep the gear from getting wet," she added dryly as she lowered herself onto the bow seat. "Then, SIT DOWN!"

Sheila followed my suggestion that she start off paddling bow. She quickly developed a strong, efficient stroke, keeping her blade low and parallel to the glassy surface. Beads of droplets sparkled in the sunlight as she moved her paddle forward before plunging the blade into the water. I picked out a point on the opposite shore and used the J stroke to keep us on course.

"You're doing great!" I said. "Are you sure you've never done this before?"

"Maybe in another life!" answered Sheila.

"OK, let's turn around. Use your draw stroke. Do you remember it?"

"I think so!"

She did and together we swung the canoe around.

We drifted and watched the progress of the other canoes. Most were making headway, but one canoe circled endlessly. Eventually, ripples from their fruitless efforts encased the boat. Nancy and Dorcas made their way over to the hapless neophytes and offered gentle coaching, but to no avail. So Nancy grabbed the bow line – the painter – and together they towed the couple to shore. No one laughed.

Back on shore we loaded all our gear, two backpacks to a canoe, and set off down Long Lake. Nancy and Dorcas split up. Each of their canoes carried one of the circling women in the bow while they paddled stern. After several hours our stalwart group rounded a point of land where the lake narrowed, and ran headlong into… ice.

Over PB & J sandwiches and oranges, the last fresh fruit of the journey, we sat cross-legged in a circle while our two instructors laid out the plan. They'd received a report the previous day before we set out that the lake might still have spots that were iced-in. Nancy spoke first. "We'll spend a couple of hours here and let the sun work on the ice, before heading out. We'll probably be able to break through with our paddles and once the lake widens again," nodding to the topographical map she held high in both hands, "the water should be open. No big deal."

"So let's do some in-depth introductions," added Dorcas. "We really haven't had a chance to do that yet."

One-by-one each woman spoke and I began to appreciate the diversity of our group. We students came from various walks of life and ranged in age from 30 to 49. One was an OB nurse and farmer from Lyme, NH, one a cop from New York City. One woman had been on the initial DOBC adult women's course and enjoyed herself so much she'd signed up again. Several had never camped or been in a canoe. One woman came decked out in entirely new clothes and gear recently purchased from L.L. Bean. She also carried two dimes with her, hoping she might come across a pay phone so she could call her husband! Two women from Rhode Island were a couple – but that took me a while to figure out. Several of us were wives and mothers.

I paid particular attention, as Marion, the fourth member of my tent group, along with Nancy and Dorcas, spoke. A petite woman with short grey hair, and lively blue eyes set in a weathered face, Marion was the oldest student on the course as well as the veteran from the initial adult woman's course. A staunch environmentalist, she had already gained some notoriety through her efforts to clean up the heavily polluted Nashua River which flowed less than a mile from her home in Massachusetts. As she spoke, I listened in awe. Here was a woman who, in addition to marriage and raising three children, had staked out a piece of life to call her own. Immediately, I saw her as a role model.

When my turn came, I spoke first about my three sons, beginning with Steve. I enthusiastically described our year in Hanover and explained our family would be returning to Long Island at summer's end. Nancy broke in.

"How do you feel about leaving Hanover?" she asked.

"Not good," I admitted. "I love living in Northern New England, and the school year for Steve has been amazing. Mike and Josh are thriving and enjoying many of the activities which meant so much to me growing up. I really don't want to leave." Nancy looked at me, a quizzical expression on her face. I realized that, for the first time, I had articulated the thought I'd kept deep inside my heart and mind.

Introductions completed, we packed up and reviewed some of the strokes again. "OK, ladies," said Nancy, "it's time to hit the water…or should I say the ice! I want everyone to switch positions, stern to bow and bow to stern. Let's go!"

Back out on the water, we drifted as the other pairs of women settled into their canoes. "Should we wait for everyone?" asked Sheila.

"Nope, let's head for the ice and start breaking a pathway. This will be fun!"

The cool air coming off the ice contrasted with the warm rays of sun streaming down from the cloudless sky. Clad in worn jeans, with the long sleeves of my chambray shirt poking through the holes of my life jacket and a blue and white striped wool hat perched on my head, we continued pounding our way through the ice-choked lake.

Suddenly Sheila raised her voice in song. " '*I am woman, hear me roar.*' "[1]

---

1    Reddy, Helen. "I Am Woman Lyrics." *Metrolyrics*. Universal Music Publishing, May 1971. Web. 23 Feb. 2016.

"*In numbers too big to ignore,*'" I responded.

Together we continued, "'And *I know too much to go back an' pretend./Cause I've heard it all before/And I've been down there on the floor/No one's ever gonna keep me down again.*"'

I smiled as sweat trickled down my face. From behind us the voices of other women chimed in.

"'*Oh yes, I am wise/But it's wisdom born of pain/Yes, I've paid the price/But look how much I've gained./If I have to, I can do anything/I am strong/I am invincible/I am woman!*'"

After a full day of paddling, in and out of ice, Nancy and Dorcas directed us to a campsite two thirds down Long Lake. Overnight a strong breeze developed and by the time we awoke in the morning, the ice was gone. Fickle weather, sun, followed by rain, followed by sun, tracked us as we settled into a daily rhythm. We awoke to the singing of birds, built a fire and cooked our bulgur breakfast. While we ate, Nancy and Dorcas brought out topo maps and the group planned the day's route.

Each morning we became a little more proficient at breaking camp and stuffing everything into our Duluth packs. Named after the Minnesota city where they are still made today, these backpacks, shaped like an oversized canvas envelope, are a traditional portaging pack. A set of thin leather straps and buckles cinch the top flap closed. Wide canvas shoulder straps and a tumpline, worn over your forehead, are used to carry gear between bodies of water or around rapids and falls too dangerous to attempt. On the water the Duluth pack's square contour allows for a comfortable fit in the bottom of a canoe. But that didn't make it any easier to swing these loaded behemoths into the boat.

"Work as a team, ladies! Grab the pack by the opposite edges of the flap, not the shoulder straps! Then on the count of three, swing 'er in!" Nancy and Dorcas shouted this reminder to us over and over. A few of us managed to perfect the technique by the end of the course.

Each day we paddled with a different partner, and alternated between bow and stern positions. For lunch we rafted-up and passed around cheese, salty summer sausage, dried fruit and an apparently endless supply of individually wrapped hard candies. Folks quickly passed me, the only licorice-lover, any ebony nuggets they unwittingly pulled from the blue nylon stuff sack, quickly christened "Sweet Sally."

My tongue began to turn black. To quench our thirst, we simply dipped our tin cups into the lake and let the cool liquid trickle down our throats. I'd never tasted better water.

After two days on Long Lake we encountered our first portage, a short one leading to the Raquette River in the popular High Peaks area of the Park. For the next several hours the swift current of the north-flowing stream, swollen with the winter snow melt, pulled us along. Towering mountains, many still topped with icy hats, lined this "Highway of the Adirondacks." Pine sentinels stood watch on sandy, deserted banks. A solitary great blue heron marched bent-kneed along a pebbled shallow, looking for dinner.

Without warning, three blasts of a whistle, the signal for danger or help, broke the silence and jolted me from the hypnotic trance of continuous paddling. Nancy, in the lead canoe, lifted her paddle overhead, and motioned for the rest of us to head towards her. We rafted up and she spoke.

"Listen carefully everyone…Try to keep the canoes from banging against each other…That's better…Do you hear anything different?"

I leaned forward, cupping one ear with my hand. And then I heard it…a muted murmur, like the noise of a distant highway.

"That sound you hear means we're approaching the Raquette River Falls. Follow closely behind me and hug the shoreline. Pretty soon we should come to a clearing that marks the carry around the falls. We'll take out there."

The somber tone of her voice left no doubt in our minds; we needed to follow her directions explicitly. Once safely on land, Nancy informed us that the carry trail ran for a mile and a half around two sets of falls. We would need to make that portage several times to get the canoes and all our gear past the falls to the campground waiting just below the falls. Our group uttered a collective groan as we learned what lay ahead, and voted to have lunch first.

As we ate, Nancy came over and squatted down beside me. "We're going to teach everyone how to do a double carry. But, I was thinking, do you want to try a solo carry?"

I'd watched both Nancy and Dorcas each lift a canoe up onto their knees and then in a single fluid motion flip the 70-plus-pound boat upside down over their head and let the crossed paddles jammed under the forward thwart settle on their shoulders. I marveled at the ease with which each woman did this.

I hesitated before answering. "Yeah, I'd like to try, but I

41

don't think I have the upper body strength to lift and flip like you do."

"Don't sell yourself short," replied Nancy. "I can help you get the canoe up. But I know you are strong enough for a solo carry." Then a sly smile crossed her face. "Besides, I've seen you watching both Dorcas and me. I know you want to try this."

I did need help with the lift and flip, but once the canoe balanced, I set off. I realized that with the stern tilted back I could see where I was going. Nancy, carrying another canoe, followed along behind me, ready to help lower my bow onto a tree notch in case I needed to rest. But I didn't. I felt strong and empowered, even as sweat stung my eyes and my shoulders began to ache. In a zone, I sang softly to myself as I moved along the pine needle carpeted path.

*"'You can bend but never break me/Cause it only serves to make me/More determined to achieve my final goal./And I come back even stronger/Not a novice any longer/'Cause you've deepened the conviction in my soul.'"*

At the end of the portage, Nancy helped lower the canoe off my shoulders. "Nice work," she said softly. I grinned and turned back for one of our Duluth packs.

As the sun lowered behind the mountains we set up camp below the falls. I joined a small group of adventurous skinny-dippers for an invigorating swim in the river. Before falling asleep, I wrote in the journal I'd begun when we landed in Hanover the previous August, the one I'd titled, "The Dream Year."

*"I am so psyched for this whole experience! My adrenalin is really pumping and I just go, go, go. It is hard at night to relax, but I think I know why I feel this way. It's like I've waited for 20-25 years for a chance*

*to really test myself physically and I may never get this chance again. The more stress there is the harder I drive myself...and I like it!"*

The next morning, we played with our canoes in the rapids, paddling into the current, and then letting the rushing waters propel us backwards. After lunch we continued down the river. The sun played peek-a-boo and then the clouds closed in. We left the High Peaks area and the pines behind us and the river slithered and wound through the surrounding low, marshy land lined with bare hardwoods. Our group made camp at Axton Landing just as a violent thunderstorm hit. We cooked and pitched our tents in a driving rain. Red and white cans of Genesee beer littered the campsite - evidently a popular gathering spot for local teens. Once the rain stopped, several of us got busy cleaning up their mess. After all, Outward Bound courses always included a community service component.

By now we'd been on the water for three days and covered close to 40 miles. Ahead lay Tupper Lake and a portage into Bridge Brook Pond, our solo site. As the last crimson and purple streaks of a spectacular sunset faded and darkness dropped like a blanket, Nancy reached into the back pocket of her pants and pulled out a worn copy of Anne Morrow Lindbergh's <u>Gift From The Sea.</u> Sparks shot from our campfire, and she began reading aloud.

*"I find there is a quality to being alone that is most precious. Life rushes back into the void, richer, more vivid, fuller than before...Women need solitude to find again the true essence of themselves...Woman must come of age by herself...she must find her true center alone...What matters is that one be for a time inwardly attentive."*

Nancy continued to talk about the solo experience, and

I felt a knot, born of anxiety, form in my stomach. I shifted uneasily and looked down at the ground. I understood when I signed up that this event would happen. Solo is the keystone of every Outward Bound course. Juxtaposed alongside the physicality wilderness travel, solo offers time for rest and reflection. Time to take stock. Time to make sense of the experience on an individual basis. But I had pushed this knowledge aside. The effort of constant movement fulfilled me. I liked expending my physical energy. But emotional energy? Confronting the demons deep inside me? The ones I refused to let surface?

Nancy finished talking and asked for questions. A cocoon of silence wrapped around us broken by the crackling and popping of the fire. One by one, folks started moving toward their tents until just our tent group – Nancy, Dorcas and Marion remained. I stared into the flames and began to cry. I cried for my sister Carol's untimely death of lupus at age 21. I cried for Steve's birth. Not for the extra chromosome which, I believed, contributed to the sweet, funny kid I loved. No, I wept for the inoperable congenital heart defect which left Steve short of breath at times and unable to participate with his brothers in some of the family's activities. And I cried for myself – the woman who, despite being married, often felt alone, the woman afraid of finding her true essence. The hot tears cracked the tough veneer protecting my interior vulnerable self. My tent mates gathered around and held me close. I could feel their energy and their caring.

Later in our tent, Marion asked me probing questions, suggesting that I try searching for answers during my solo. What did I really want from life? What was missing from my relationship with Roger? What values did I hold most dearly? My eye lids began to droop and, emotionally exhausted, I fell into a deep, dreamless sleep.

In the morning, our six canoes beat their way down Tupper Lake, into a stiff headwind. With Marion in the stern, I put my head down and paddled hard as our canoe bounced up and down in the frothy waves. A mist began falling and the lake closed in. Marion understood and respected my need for silence.

"Eeyaw!" Dorcas's voice carried over the water and we turned toward the sound. Along the shoreline, she had spotted the faint trail marking the carry into Bridge Brook Pond.

As I carried our canoe over the seemingly undisturbed portage, I kept my eyes down and thought of Robert Frost's famous line, *"And both that morning equally lay/In leaves no step had trodden black."* I wondered if we were the first people to make our way into the pond this spring.

A large clearing, marked the end of the portage and we began to fill the space with canoes and gear – base camp. We ate a late lunch and listened intently while our leaders issued final instructions. "Besides your sleeping bag and Therm-a-Rest, you'll each get a tarp, some rope and a hatchet. You'll have to figure out how to use these materials to create a shelter. That should be your first order of business," explained Nancy. "You'll have a limited, but adequate, supply of food and a waterproof container with about a dozen matches." She held up a metal cylinder with a hinged screw-top and demonstrated how to use the rough side to strike a match. "Use these sparingly," she cautioned. "Once they're gone, you won't be getting anymore."

"What about toilet paper?" asked one woman. Each campsite in the Park had come equipped with a well-stocked outhouse.

"Well, we brought a few rolls of TP and you can take some if you want," replied Nancy. "But you'll have to pack it out, including the used stuff."

Several women shuddered.

Dorcas chimed in. "Remember the reading from Anne Lindbergh. We really encourage you to keep things as simple as you feel you can. We'll teach you how to make a cat-hole. The hole should be about 6-8 inches deep and well away from any water. You will fill it in before you leave. Consider doing solo without your toothbrush, toothpaste, soap and toilet paper. BUT if you do take toilet paper, you WILL pack it out. Tampons, too. (Several women were menstruating, not an unusual occurrence when a group of females gather together for an extended period of time.)

I headed off to collect my things and myself. I dug my sleeping bag and pad out of the Duluth pack along with an extra sweater, sweatpants and my wool hat. Then I opened the small yellow nylon sack which held my essentials, dumped everything onto the pine-needled ground, and began to sort the contents into two piles. Into the "take" pile went my journal, two pens, and my jackknife – the one Roger had given me for my 38th birthday. I had no problem placing my toothbrush, toothpaste and soap in the "leave behind" pile. Natural substances could replace those. The same with toilet paper. My eyes landed on the watch on my left wrist. Leave my watch? How would I know when the kids would be leaving for or returning from school? Or when Roger was fixing them dinner? Or putting them to bed? With a sigh I unbuckled the black cloth strap and removed my last remaining link to my life in Hanover. I glanced at the pale thin line on my wrist, evidence indeed that I had spent almost a week living outdoors. OK, I thought, it's time to be alone, really alone.

Back at the base camp clearing I stood to the side, a dull ache in my stomach, and watched our numbers dwindle. One-by-one the women paddled off with either Nancy or Dorcus to be dropped at solo sites, spread around the perimeter of the pond. Nancy saved me for her last passenger. Paddling across the still water, neither of us spoke. She nosed the canoe up to the spot she'd scouted and got out to help me with my gear. Then she gave me a hug along with a warm smile and offered, "You'll do fine, Linda." With that Nancy pivoted, stepped into the canoe and pushed off. I stood silently as I watched her paddle away, trailing an ever-widening V wake. I grabbed my gear and climbed up the steep bank to begin my solo.

Atop the bank, I dropped my gear and looked around. I resisted the temptation to turn towards the water and catch one last glimpse of Nancy's canoe. I found myself in a small rectangular clearing, the ground matted with dead grass and leaves. To one side was the level remains of what had once been a sizeable pine tree, and next to that a stone fire ring left by a previous camper. That stump will make a good table, I thought. A large boulder deposited during some ancient ice age, rested on the shoreline, its sloping edge dropping into the water. Hmmm…if the sun shines tomorrow that will be a great place to sunbath. Turning in the other direction, I spied a patch of spongy moss, just big enough to place a sleeping bag. Evidence of beaver activity abounded and I noticed several saplings, with tell-tale tooth marks at one end lying on the ground. Perhaps they might come in handy as I constructed my shelter. Beyond the clearing, stood the Adirondack wilderness – an impenetrable mixture of pines and bare-branched hardwoods. I looked skyward and noticed the sun's position. Soon it would dip behind the tree line. Time to get busy.

I shook out my tarp and placed it on the patch of moss. As I stared at the rectangular shape, a vision of a three-sided prism with open ends formed in my mind. I refolded the clear material the long way into three equal sections, paced off the length, and headed for the beaver's workplace. I easily found three fallen limbs of the right size, dragged them back to the tarp and positioned two of the poles along each side of the first third of the plastic cloth. I lay my sleeping bag between the poles on what would be the shelter's floor. Hatchet in hand, I stepped into the edge of the woods searching for two sturdy Y-shaped branches. Back in the clearing, I sharpened the ends of each branch into a point and using the hatchet's head, pounded the notch where the branches veered into the ground at the foot and head of my bedding. Balancing the third pole in the notches of the Y-supports, I carefully lifted the remaining two-thirds of the tarp over the ridge pole and down the other side. Next I opened my jackknife and cut short lengths of rope for guy-lines to steady the branches holding the ridgepole. I splayed the guy-lines out from the two Y-branches and tied them securely to my tent stakes - thin, strong limbs I'd cut and sharpened at one end and then pounded into the ground. I used smaller pieces of rope, along with additional stakes, to secure the long, open edge of the shelter and lined that edge with rocks as well. I checked all around for stability and tightness. Then I stood back, sweating profusely, to admire my work. Pretty slick, I said silently.

That evening I struck one of my precious matches against the match container and touched the blazing end to the collection of twigs and birch-bark strips I'd arranged in the fire ring. I wondered again who had been there before me. I patiently fed the conflagration from my stack of logs and then sat back, cross-legged, staring into my campfire. Above me the night had arrived in formal attire, diamonds sparkled against black velvet. I nibbled on a piece of hardtack and drank some water. This isn't so bad, I concluded. What was I so afraid of? Eventually, as I began to shiver in the rapidly cooling evening, I doused the glowing embers, and headed for my shelter. Slowly and very carefully, like a snake re-inhabiting her skin, I crawled into my prism-shaped tent. I squiggled down deep into my bag, zipped the side up to my chin and closed my eyes. The eerie call of a loon lulled me to sleep.

The next morning the Goddesses blessed each solitary woman with a perfect day. I remained in my sleeping bag, snug and warm, and began reading from the first page of my Dream Year journal – dated 8/20/77. As I relived our time in Hanover, a singular thought kept pounding in my brain: Shit, I really don't want to return to Port Jefferson. Can I find a way for our family to stay in Hanover? Dare I disturb the universe? Eventually, I eased my way out of my cocoon, and stretched, soaking up the sun's rays streaming through the pines ringing the shoreline. I stripped off my clothes and using sand and cool water, scrubbed them along with myself. Then, draping my dripping laundry on some low branches, I lay my naked self on the large glacial platform by the water's edge.

I remained there for a long time, alternately dozing and watching hawks circling lazily above me. Only nature's call and a grumbling stomach drove me from my perch. I sat on the stump by the fire ring pondering the questions Marion had raised about life's dreams, relationships and values. I reached for a pen and began writing in my journal – filling page after page. I moved very little. I watched a spider spin a web. I wrote some more. I opened to a back page and sketched my solo site. I filled and refilled my cup from the lake. I wrote and wrote and wrote. I took out my jackknife and tried my hand at whittling. I ate some gorp and made a half-hearted attempt at gathering more firewood…but that seemed like too much work. When I noticed goosebumps on my arms, I got dressed. I gave thanks for the lack of mosquitoes. Then I wrote, *This quiet feels so soothing. I've never been alone and in such a quiet place for so long.*

As the sun set, I sat silently watching the lake. Fish rose to feed sending ripples out in ever expanding circles on a smooth, black surface. A beaver made her way across the pond and clumsily waddled up the bank about 100 feet from me. "Sorry," I whispered. "Your spot is still occupied. Thank you for the poles you left for me. You can have them back tomorrow, I promise." A flock of geese honked their way overhead, and a slender silver crescent, appeared in the darkening sky.

In my shelter, I held my flashlight and read aloud the pages I had written – close to thirty in one day! The extended period of stillness and simplicity had worked its magic. I didn't have any answers, but I knew some truths: after high school I had done what was expected of me - go to college, get married, have children. Women in the 60's and 70's wore the title of homemakers. Husbands ran the show and earned the money. Families lived wherever the men found work. Certainly that had been our pattern.

But now, in Hanover, I'd found a place and lifestyle I loved. I'd met women who enjoyed the same activities I did: hiking, camping, running, skiing. Both Mike and Josh had many friends, and I exulted as I watched their progress in the local ski program. And Steve's year at the Ray School had succeeded beyond my wildest hopes. Finally, he'd gone to school with his brothers in the community where we lived. I didn't want him returning to the isolation of the BOCES program, and I doubted I'd have the energy or the time to fight for a change in that system. I didn't want the dream year to end. I needed to find my voice.

The woman, wife and mother who'd left home just eight days ago had dipped her toes into transformative waters, whose currents had exposed previously unseen pathways around what I had perceived as firmly positioned obstacles. I was in the process of becoming – what that would be, I couldn't yet tell. But I had climbed. I had seen. Somehow I would find a way to maintain the view from on high, to be true to myself, to care for myself, so I could care for others. Not an easy change, but I had to try. I fell asleep humming and mouthing the words to what had become MY song.

*I am woman watch me grow/See me standing toe to toe/As I spread my lovin' arms across the land/But I'm still an embryo/with a long, long way to go/Until I make my brother understand ... I am strong ... I am invincible ... I am woman...*

"Linda? Linda? Are you there?" The sound of Nancy's voice softly calling my name woke me. Morning already? Was solo over? I grinned up at her as I slithered out.

"Cool-looking shelter," she observed. "So, how did it go?"

"Pretty wonderful," I replied. "But I won't mind getting my hands on some of the luxuries I left back at base camp. I'm surprised I can talk, given the fur coating on my teeth."

Everyone was quiet and subdued as we packed up camp and portaged out of Bridge Brook Pond to Tupper Lake. Only two more days remained before our adventure ended. We waited for the DOBC van and driver over an hour at our designated pick-up spot at the end of the lake. Following the long journey back to Hanover, we pitched our tents in the ghostly darkness at the same Storrs Pond campsite we'd occupied our initial night and crawled into our sleeping bags. I lay still. To my surprise I missed my solo site. This location felt too familiar, a sure indicator that the end of the course loomed ahead. Finally, the sound of creaking limbs in towering pines lulled me to sleep.

A thin finger of sunlight wiggled through a sliver of an opening in the tent and tickled my eyelids open. After our bulgur breakfast we piled into the van and headed for the turbulent waters of Vermont's White River, which had undergone her annual transformation from gentle tubing stream to a frothy, angry sluice fed by the spring snow melt – white-water day! As I learned to see the tongues of smooth water indicating the best route between two rocks, or to head for an eddy and a brief rest before the next set of rapids, I began to feel a rhythm similar to skiing. Gee, I thought, if we stayed in the area instead of returning to Long Island, we could buy a canoe and I could teach Roger what I am learning.

Back at our campsite, for our final night together, I lingered around the fire with a few others, listening to the crackle of pine knots exploding and watching the sparks rise into the black sky and flicker out. No one said much. The pulsing embers glowed, then faded and died. In our tent, Nancy and I, and Dorcas and Marion, now all close friends, silently exchanged our evening backrubs – a nightly ritual. I fell asleep in the grip of melancholy – anxious to see my family, but sad at the prospect of this experience ending.

Our course concluded the following morning with the traditional Outward Bound "marathon." For us this meant paddling across the pond, then portaging the canoes through the woods and up a hill to Route 10 where the familiar van waited for us. After loading the canoes onto the trailer for the final time, we ran the three-plus miles into Hanover. Stoked for this final challenge, I led the rest of the women along the road and through the campus to the finish line – the Dartmouth gym where we'd first met 10 days earlier.

The hot showers felt amazing. So did the fresh clothing we donned before walking to a restaurant on Main Street where two reserved tables awaited us. Giddy with the options before us, we celebrated with drinks and food – ordered from a menu no less! As the tables were cleared by two bemused waitresses, Nancy and Dorcas stood and signaled for our attention. Nancy gave one final reading – taken from the novel *Mount Analogue* by the French author René Daumal. The powerful and poignant words she spoke seared deep into my soul and have continued to guide me throughout my life. Then Dorcas called each woman up to receive a certificate indicating our successful competition of the course along with the coveted Outward Bound pin. We saved our loudest applause for the woman with the two dimes. Laughingly, she handed them to Dorcas in exchange for her certificate. Amid hugs and tears we left the restaurant. The real world awaited us.

-----------------

Back at the gym I dropped my two dimes into the pay phone, called Roger and asked him to load the boys in our car and come take me home. Soon the maroon station wagon known as "Big Red" pulled into the parking lot, rolled to a stop and three boys tumbled out clutching homemade Mother's Day cards. Mike and Josh flung themselves into my outstretched arms and then stood back quivering with excitement.

"Mommy! You're alive!"

"Where'd you go? What'd you do?

"Did ya see any bears?"

"Did ya go swimming?"

"Where'd ya go to the bathroom?"

Steve stepped between his brothers, wrapped his arms around me and said quietly, "I miss you. I worry 'bout you." Then he nuzzled his face against my chest and held on tight.

Roger stood back waiting for his turn and when Mike and Josh quieted, he moved forward and drew me toward him. "I'm glad you're back," he said softly.

That evening, the boys in bed, we built a fire – more for atmosphere than warmth – and sat together on the living room couch sipping beers and catching up. Roger handed me two sheets of white lined paper folded in half. "This is for you," he said. "I decided to keep a journal while you were gone."

"Really?" I looked at him pop-eyed. "A journal? That's so unlike you! Have you ever kept a journal?"

Roger ducked his head shyly. "No, never. But I really missed you and this just seemed like a way to stay connected to you."

I reached over and hugged him. "You couldn't have given me a better gift. This is perfect."

As my eyes tracked down the first page, one entry stopped me short.

*"I was very depressed on Monday. I ate a lot, and I have more understanding of what you face. It's hard to keep my mind on home, meals, kids and work. Big storm tonight. Lightning, thunder, heavy rain. Where*

*and how are you?"*

Welcome to my world, I thought.

Roger tipped back his beer and drained it. "I've killed this one. I think I'll head to bed." He looked at me meaningfully.

"Yeah, I've got a few more sips here and then I'll be along."

Starting in the morning I'd begin my descent from the summit. I knew I'd need to start my campaign to stay in Hanover, and that the discussions with Roger would challenge us both. But I had tested myself physically and emotionally. I felt empowered and determined. I set my empty bottle on the kitchen counter and moved down the hallway, stopping to peek in at our sleeping sons. I murmured softly, "Sleeping in a bed is going to feel strange, with Roger, maybe even stranger."

# EVER SO SLIGHTLY

*Ever So Slightly was written just after my grandfather died. I was reflecting about life while I sat on our dock on the east side of Lake George.*

*There was something about looking at the mountains that seemed to order everything and bring perspective.*

*Cathy S. McDowell*

There are things that bend
ever so slightly forward,
like your roses
full of rain and
your gray, felt hat
while you tie up
the tomatoes.
Hot summer afternoons,
a dozen tiny cousins played tag
while I'd sit perched
on the edge of a wooden
lawn chair, one toe resting
on the top of a fat slippery
watermelon seed,
my face and chest still sticky.
You move through the garden
like a lover,
stooping to pick a
dead blossom
with a trembling hand
or dropping a
Japanese beetle

in a soup can filled with kerosene. The dahlias lean
toward
your touch
bobbing in the sun
leaving them blushing
when their row was done.
And when the storm would
finally come
I'd run barefoot
down the muddy garden path
to the strawberry patch
where you'd say, "Watch out for the runners, kiddo".
rising to follow me
brushing off your
dusty right knee.

## NINE SONNETS
*Chuck Gibson*

### Lost Pond

Where wet woods whetted all your senses clear
The dog still shivers to the bone beneath
The bare and barren broken branches here
Above green haloes on the ground, each wreath

A whorl of shiny sourgrass and fern
That drapes the forest floor but you don't know
If into sun or clouds you'll finally go.
To keep on is the only way to learn.

The mist both grips and drips as twig tips burn
With new green growth that always will repeat
And shattered trees munch crunch beneath your feet
By saturated stumps, your only seat.

But where's the force to break the forest's spell?
You might be strong enough but who can tell?

### Saranac Lake, Fourth of July

From nowhere rapids flare and spit and whirl
And hit the air and spin and skip and curl
Unfurling flags of stars spun to display
An independence day of ceaseless spray

Far from the fireworks in city parks
Where flow slows down downstream in graceful arcs.
Up here new freedom bursts its box and knocks
The door wide open breaking all the locks.

Impediments the river wears away
Turn into sediments and make a shore
Where we can see the water pour and roar
And play its best in zesty disarray.

Its freedom is so manifest to all
As if the stream were struck by cannon ball.

## Lincoln Pond
*(a dream poem)*

There was a long and narrow lake below
With wooded shores and wooden boats to row
All anchored on the water there although
Just how to reach the boats we didn't know

For there were other boats with rowers there.
I wanted to be in a boat to share
Some time with you (you whom I'm writing to),
But we would have to swim or wade, for who

Could row us to a rowboat so we'd be
Included in this blest fraternity?
There was a muscled man who by a rock
Gazed at the water. Printed out in block

Black letters LIFEGUARD graced his shirt,
But we would never see his face. That hurt.

## Long Pond

As when a bowl of white replaces night
Below with glow of tintype tints all bright,
And light that painted panes with pinkish hues
Refracts to fire red and bloody blues,

So life can brighten over window sill
By pond in morning lying quiet still,
Where light is pouring into it and will,
Discerning good replacing chill until

The dogs swim out to buoys made of wood
And try to bring them back. They can't. They should
Have learned, but not like people they've been burned.
Perhaps they think contentment must be earned.

The dawn that seemed a miracle and more
To me, to them means only ceaseless chore.

### When I was Leaving Church in the Foyer…
*(a dream poem)*

When I was leaving church in the foyer
The pastor said to wait to get my child,
The one we had adopted yesterday,
Who now was in a backpack, papers filed.

I walked outside and felt so full of life;
Upon my back the quiet baby lay,
But now I couldn't seem to find my wife;
She must have left the church another way.

By then she'd gone, and home was very far.
My son slept on my lap without a sound,
When we rode on the bus. She had the car.
The streets seemed unfamiliar way downtown.

Without my wife I did not feel so well
There sitting on the bed at the motel.

## Champlain
*(a dream poem)*


Canoeing north with you we came to where
The river widened to a lake and there
Appeared a bridge ahead and underneath we went
Into a land of light where soon we saw

More lights onshore where some kind of event
Was going on. We steered that way with awe
For everything was new. It was a fair
With music. People mingled and were kind.

I browsed inside a shop so I could find
An item that might tell me where I was.
Come stay, a gentle woman said, because
You must be lost. I left the fair behind
And to an attic room was soon assigned.

Into a brass and comfy bed I fell
But I could tell you were nearby and well.

## Ausable Flume

Where water white met pool of green I saw
A rocky shelf where water rubbed rock raw
In flood time long ago to then withdraw
And leave laid bare a landscape once a maw

Of maelstrom in mind's eye: this floor in spots
Is dotted now with pools reflecting lots
Of smashed up trees amidst the mushy blots
Of slimy moss and slippery mush, but one

Abandoned channel yields more clarity:
Touched now by new and rosy light of sun,
Some stones are buffed to gold. Here one can see
New beauty where all else was left undone.

Catastrophe of flood through flume reveals
New gold the river usually conceals.

**Discovery Mountain**

One day we climbed Discovery and found
A spur of rock that left the top and wound
On down a rippled ridge the rock had crowned
As if earth's stony spine had burst the ground

Amidst the woods so silent all around
Where flower carpets recently unrolled
Revealed new trillium released from cold
And as a good book long ago had told

Expressed more beauty than a bag of gold.
So white the lilies were but balanced by
New baby blooms far bluer than the sky.
We rested on the rock and wondered why

Upon this crest so high we'd been so blest
To make a memory among our very best.

## Upper Boquet

Some sounds are like a cascade falling
In shady shadowed forest sunk in sleep,
While others from deep pools are calling
Sad songs to sandy beach by ferny seep.

These voices sing and ring and linger longing
To wade where sunny trail swings out and wide,
A symphony of roaring river sprawling,
While thrump of grouse from thickets where they hide

Adds a percussive sound to woods belonging,
A window into nature's freedom feeling,
So different from the wall and floor and ceiling,
Confining, stiff and stifling, stunted and concealing.

You've stumbled on a wild open door
Where rivers reeling tumble ever more.

## SUN TEA

*Cathy S. McDowell*

The other night, in the darkness, without bothering to turn on a light, I found my way to the bathroom. Following the smooth wall to the edge of my bedroom door, feeling for the hinge (so I knew it was open) to make the sharp turn into the bathroom. I used to leave the night light on in there but either the holes in the screen have widened or bugs have morphed smaller because my sink would be full of tiny dead bodies in the morning.

So it was dark everywhere. Which is okay. When we moved to the quiet east side of Lake George over 50 years ago, there were no street lights on our road. That was city stuff. Eventually, our two neighbors agreed some light would be nice so we split the Ni-Mo bill three ways each month. Luxury has its price.

So I say all that to clarify that being in the dark is not scary for me. I've always found clarity of vision in this place snuggled hen-like near the base of Buck Mountain. There's something primal in the balance of things here. Twilight and dawn. Light and darkness. We kids used to call the beginning of summer "*the time when the sky turned upside down.*" Lightening bugs. Tiny constellations all over the grass or mapping out ancient invocations on our porch screens. Ordinary unnoticeable brown things by day. Prophetic luminaries by night.

So I am comfortable with the darkness and often find myself better off with my eyes closed. I have my life memorized and, for the most part, it serves me well.

Except last Wednesday night when I got up to go the bathroom because I had been drinking too much sun tea. Freshly brewed on the deck railing with a few sprigs of wild spearmint. It was a mesmerizing ritual as tea bags leaked honey brown ribbons into the warm water and the mint tangled in flavor. Which explains why I am up at 3AM on my way to the bathroom in the dark.

There is a danger, I've found, in thinking that life is predictable. When it becomes most familiar, it often, like a resolute stream, changes course without notice in pursuit of a different way around non-negotiable things.

My house has remained the same with a few modern add-ons to its 100 year old frame. My bed is in the same position under the slanted knee walls. My door is still on hinges and not been changed to one of those fancy pocket doors. My hand accurately knows the length on my footboard. And I know when to turn, the measured steps after and the hop back into bed.

But I made an error in judgment by believing that something I had just left would be the same when I returned - all based on my empirical truth, of course. But not tonight. As I felt my way back through the darkness my left hand gliding across the wicker footboard, turning left, taking three steps and then free falling face down onto my bed, there was a miscalculation. Some cosmic misalignment. An archeological uplifting along a geographic fault line. Unanticipated. Like when my washing machine goes out of balance for the second load but not the first. Or my table rocks at lunch but not at breakfast. And I began to think, mid-air, that perhaps the sun was involved. I had perceived it as a simple brewing process. But there must have been more. I should have been a better sentinel.

So the long and short of this sun tea intoxication - possession - hostile take-over story is that my face dive was not as planned, based on my experience, and I hit the headboard instead of my soft impressionable mattress. Having not opened my eyes through the entire trek (in Helen-Keller fashion), the sudden pain I felt on my forehead was more dreamlike than awakening. Like remembering pain but it wasn't mine. I recall thinking *Maybe I have a concussion? I'm not supposed to go to sleep. I could die.* But sleep was sweeter.

When I showered the next day and was drying my hair, I noticed a purple bruise on my forehead accompanied by a small bump and dried blood. I wondered where it had come from. Then I remembered that the sky up here in the Adirondacks turns upside down in June.

**2 HAIKUS**

*Mary L. Randall*


Bird bath, cement tub
Bright feathers in a frenzy
Of fluttering wings


Written 1968


Wilbur and Orville
felt sure they were born to soar
Oh, trans-species Wrights!


Written 2016

# THE NATURE OF PLACE
### Charles Watts

There is a place of great beauty, nestled in the foothills of high mountains in central Oregon, through which a river flows. My grandfather had a farm there. As a child, I played in the river and once was swept away, saved at the last gasp by a father tormented that he had not kept an eye on me at every moment. There were no dry clothes for me, so I was wrapped in a cousin's dress. Mom dragged out the Kodak Brownie and snapped me frowning and wet, my four year old manhood destroyed. The photo of that humiliation is, I hope, forever lost.

When my father went to war, the rest of our family moved there to wait out the armistice, then moved on to wherever his assignments took us...California, Germany, Georgia, Florida, Missouri, Japan, Montana...and each time we moved, the trinkets and treasure we had acquired in each new place were sent to the town and stored in a rented shed, watched over by my grandparents and awaiting our return. When my father retired, he bought a place in the beautiful town, unpacked the shed, built a house to hold his memories, and gave the last thirty years of his life to the local Masons and Eastern Star and Veterans of Foreign Wars. My mother found a job as assistant to the district congresswoman, her first paid work since marriage. It gave her an identity she had always lacked, a place in society outside the shadow of her husband, The Colonel. They both became a part of the community and made it their home after lives filled with travel and adventure.

When my brother was killed, much too early, by a

drunk driver, he was buried in the local cemetery, near our grandparents. When dad died, he was buried there. When mom died, she, too, was buried next to the ones she loved. I continued the migratory behaviour I learned as a youth, with stops in Iran and Afghanistan and Malaysia and Indonesia and Costa Rica and six different states. I surrendered to my wanderlust and wandered the world, but never did I find a place where I felt rooted, never did I feel I had finally found my place.

If ever there was a town I should feel was my home, the resting place of my parents and grandparents and brother, the scene of my youthful vacations and early childhood, should have been it. In a moment of mid-life crisis, I tried to make it so. I moved there with my children and spent a year. I met no person there who had ever written a poem or painted a picture or felt the need to understand what the outside world was like. No one remotely like me. The lumber mill had closed and half the town was out of work and on welfare and most were drunks or druggies and most seemed OK with that. None seemed to want to make a better life. I hated the town and its people and its ambiance and its ethos and left as soon as life made that possible. I only go back to visit the graves of my ancestors.

Much later in our journey, my wife and I inherited a house in the Adirondacks from her brother, who passed away unexpectedly from a brain tumor. I had been there twice, each for a week-long visit. She had visited the area many times as a youth, had even stayed at her brother's place and been a spectator at the 1980 Olympics, but had never thought of living in such a cold and wild place. Minus thirty in January was just not her thing. We found someone to rent the place that first winter, then decided to retire early and spend the cold months in the high desert of Arizona and the hot as Hades months in the high peaks.

The first summer we decided to dig in and give the place a real chance to become a part of our lives. We got the local guidebook to cultural events and went to every concert and art opening and play and poetry reading on offer. We met people and talked to them and became friends and were invited to dinner and invited people into our home. We hiked and planted a garden and made a few changes around the house and tried to make it our own. We did what my parents had done when they moved to Oregon...became a part of the life of the town.

After a few years, I became bored with retirement and took a job teaching at the local community college. I had not been a teacher for 35 years, but somehow convinced the department head I was worth a try, despite my lack of recent experience. I made a new community of friends and found a new purpose for my days. My wife did the same, reviving her interest in the visual arts and becoming a printmaker. The Adirondacks had become a real home. I stayed to teach in the winters, and my wife traveled back and forth between Arizona and New York, still not happy with the barbarity of winter.

We did not marry to spend lots of time apart. After some soul searching, we decided the house in Arizona was too far away, so we sold it and bought a place in South Carolina, only a two day commute, and went back to spending winters in the warmth of a different south and summers in the cool of the mountains. After two winters in Charleston, we began talking about whether to keep the house in the mountains or sell it and spend the summers on vacation in Europe, South America, Asia, travelling and seeing more of the world before we got too old to wander. We would spend one more summer in the Adirondacks and make our decision.

What is it about a place that makes it feel like home? The stomping grounds of my youth, the old family home in the west, had my history in its palm, but did not sing to my heart. My new home in the high peaks of upstate New York invited me in and greeted me with new friends who cared about the things of this world that gave me both hope and pleasure, poetry and art and caring about the land and the world and the nature of joy. My parents found their happiness in a small town in Oregon, with people they could relate to, even if I couldn't. I had found mine in a small town in New York in a place my parents would have found totally alien. Would I now abandon that happiness for an uncharted future?

We returned to our personal mountain, the back side of Heaven Hill, on June 2. I had told my wife that, since she had inherited the house, it was her decision to keep it or sell. I didn't have a horse in that race, but I did have my hopes. On the morning of June 3, my wife told me she woke up and looked at the trees and smelled the air and remembered all the friends she had here, and that she didn't want to abandon this place. We could travel for a month or two whenever and wherever we wanted, but this ground felt like home. I quietly rejoiced, went to the kitchen, and fried her some blueberry flapjacks with maple syrup made by a friend up the road.

**OUR WRITERS:**

Linda Morrow
(memoir)  WHAT AM I, CHOPPED LIVER?
*Navigating a Path for My Son Born
with Down Syndrome in 1966*

Mary L. Randall
(fiction/poetry)  GHOST OF STARBUCKVILLE DAM

Charles Watts
(fiction)  RAPTURES
(poetry)  WAKING UP IN A BEAUTIFUL ROOM

Cathy S. McDowell
(Social Justice)  THE WAITING PLACE

Chuck Gibson
(poetry)  FORTY FALLS,
           SEVEN STORMS,
                THIRTY THREE SONNETS

Judith Dow Moore
(poetry)  12993